ZOMBIE ANIMALS
PARASITES TAKE CONTROL!

ZOMBIE FISH

BY JOLENE ALESSI

Gareth Stevens
PUBLISHING

Please visit our website, www.garethstevens.com. For a free color catalog of all our high-quality books, call toll free 1-800-542-2595 or fax 1-877-542-2596.

Library of Congress Cataloging-in-Publication Data

Alessi, Jolene.
Zombie fish / by Jolene Alessi.
p. cm. — (Zombie animals: parasites take control!)
Includes index.
ISBN 978-1-4824-2840-7 (pbk.)
ISBN 978-1-4824-2841-4 (6 pack)
ISBN 978-1-4824-2842-1 (library binding)
1. Parasites — Juvenile literature. 2. Host-parasite relationships — Juvenile literature. 3. Fishes — Juvenile literature. I. Title.
QL617.2 A44 2016
597—d23

First Edition

Published in 2016 by
Gareth Stevens Publishing
111 East 14th Street, Suite 349
New York, NY 10003

Designer: Samantha DeMartin
Editor: Kristen Rajczak

Photo credits: Cover, pp. 1, 15 DEA/F. BALLANTI/De Agostini/Getty Images; p. 5, Juan Gaertner/Shutterstock.com; pp. 7, 21 (stickleback) CreativeNature R.Zwerver/Shutterstock.com; pp. 9, 21 (kingfisher) AFP/DPA/Getty Images; pp. 11, 21 (copepod) Jubal Harshaw/Shutterstock.com; p. 13 Leo Leo/Picture Press/Getty Images; p. 17 Craig Banner/fishpathogens.net; p. 19 Gregory Johnston/Shutterstock.com; p. 20 Tania Zbrodko/Shutterstock.com.

Printed in the United States of America

CPSIA compliance information: Batch #CS15GS: For further information contact Gareth Stevens, New York, New York at 1-800-542-2595.

CONTENTS

Words in the glossary appear in **bold** type the first time they are used in the text.

PARASITISM

Parasites are **organisms** that live in, on, or with another living thing. Scientists believe parasites make up about 50 percent of the living things on Earth. Not all affect their hosts in the same way. Often, parasites harm their hosts. They may even kill them!

Many parasites only have one kind of host in their lifetime. A tapeworm called *Schistocephalus solidus* has three! One of them is the stickleback fish. *S. solidus* does more than live inside the stickleback—it turns the fish into a zombie!

TAKE-OVER TRUTHS

A HOST IS THE ORGANISM A PARASITE LIVES IN, ON, OR WITH.

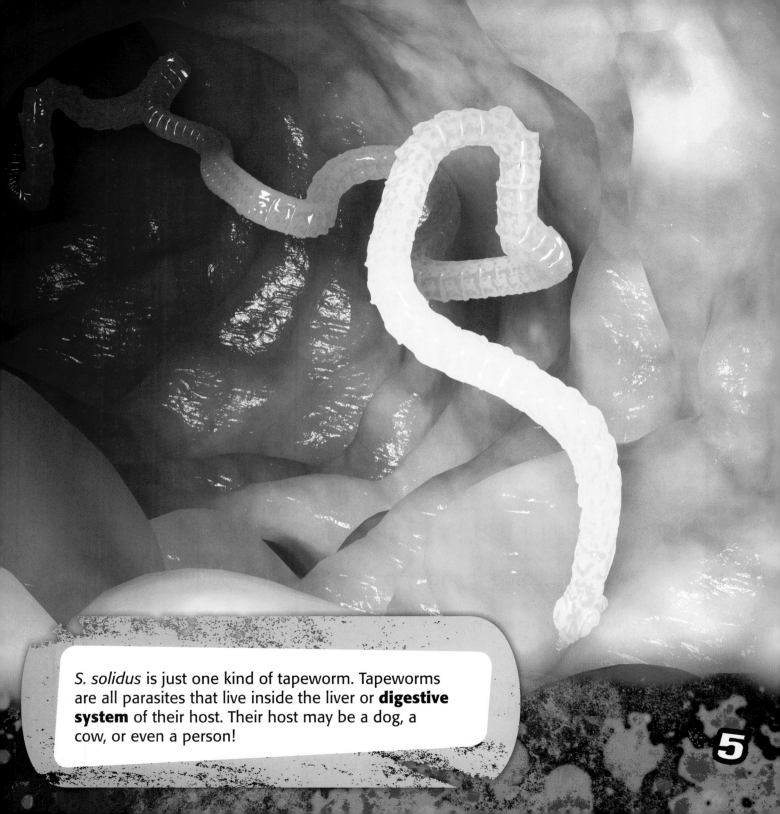

S. solidus is just one kind of tapeworm. Tapeworms are all parasites that live inside the liver or **digestive system** of their host. Their host may be a dog, a cow, or even a person!

STICKLEBACK

Sticklebacks are small fish that only grow to be about 7 inches (18 cm) long. Along their back are two to 16 **spines**. Of the eight species, or kinds, of stickleback, some are named for the number of spines they have, such as the three-spined stickleback and the nine-spined stickleback.

Sticklebacks don't have scales like other fish. Instead, their body is covered with thin, bony plates. These fish come in many colors, including white, brown, and green.

TAKE-OVER TRUTHS

MANY KINDS OF STICKLEBACKS ARE FOUND
IN NORTH AMERICAN WATERS.

Sticklebacks may live in freshwater or salt water. They're also found in brackish water, which occurs where salty ocean water meets a body of freshwater.

STEP ONE

The stickleback is only one part in *S. solidus's* journey. In fact, *S. solidus* just uses the stickleback to reach its definitive, or final, host—a water bird. That's also where this parasite begins life. *S. solidus* lays eggs inside its bird host's digestive system. The eggs leave the host bird in its waste, usually near water.

In the water, the eggs **hatch** into larvae. The larvae are eaten by copepods, which are a kind of **crustacean**. The copepods are *S. solidus's* first host.

TAKE-OVER TRUTHS

S. SOLIDUS LIVES WHEREVER ITS HOSTS ARE! IT'S FOUND IN MUCH OF NORTH AMERICA, INCLUDING ALASKA AND PARTS OF CANADA, AND IN EUROPE AND ASIA.

There are about 40 different kinds of birds that *S. solidus* can **infect**, including kingfishers, gulls, and terns. They all live near the water and feed on fish.

9

INTO THE FISH

How does *S. solidus* get into the gut of a stickleback? The stickleback eats an infected copepod! The stickleback is the tapeworm's intermediate, or middle, host.

S. solidus looks different when it infects the copepod and when it infects the stickleback. Inside the copepod, *S. solidus* **develops** into a long, solid larva with hooks on one end. Once inside the stickleback, the parasite loses the body part with the hooks. It develops body parts that get rid of waste and others used for **reproduction.**

A STICKLEBACK CAN HAVE MORE THAN ONE, BUT LIKELY NO MORE THAN FOUR, *S. SOLIDUS* INFECTIONS.

Copepods are food for many kinds of fish, not just sticklebacks. They're tiny organisms that live in oceans around the world.

PARASITE IN CHARGE

Once inside the stickleback, *S. solidus* needs to grow. However, it needs to be sure the stickleback doesn't know it's been infected by a parasite! How *S. solidus* stops the stickleback's body from attacking it isn't known.

It's also not known how *S. solidus* changes the stickleback's **behavior**. The stickleback becomes a zombie! It swims alone and won't try to get away from a predator. This is all because *S. solidus* wants the fish to be eaten by a bird!

TAKE-OVER TRUTHS

S. SOLIDUS FEEDS ON PARTS OF THE STICKLEBACK'S BODY AS WELL AS ANY FOOD THE STICKLEBACK TAKES IN WHILE INFECTED.

Some scientists believe *S. solidus* makes **chemicals** while inside the stickleback that allow it to control the fish's behavior.

HOT WATER

S. solidus also makes its host fish swim where the parasite wants to! Sticklebacks commonly like to swim in water that's warm—but not too warm. *S. solidus* likes it much warmer! The warmer the water, the bigger *S. solidus* can grow. And the bigger it can grow, the more eggs it can lay later.

So, sticklebacks infected with *S. solidus* head to water as warm as 68°F (20°C). That's about 8 degrees warmer than the stickleback would like. These zombie fish don't have a choice!

TAKE-OVER TRUTHS

COPEPODS INFECTED WITH *S. SOLIDUS* SEEM TO EAT MORE AND BE LESS ABLE TO GET AWAY FROM PREDATORS. COULD THESE TINY ORGANISMS BE ZOMBIES, TOO?

If this three-spined stickleback had its way, it wouldn't swim in water warmer than about 60°F (15.5°C).

MAKING ROOM AND MOVING ON

It's clear when a stickleback has a tapeworm living inside it. Its body starts to swell on the bottom where the parasite is growing in its digestive system.

S. solidus remains inside the stickleback for about 17 days, trying to get as large as possible. The zombie fish continues to carelessly swim alone near the surface so birds can see it. When one finally does, *S. solidus* has a chance to reach its final host. The tapeworm's success means its host fish's death.

TAKE-OVER TRUTHS

A MALE STICKLEBACK BUILDS A NEST FROM PLANTS AND BRINGS A FEMALE STICKLEBACK THERE TO LAY HER EGGS. STICKLEBACKS WON'T TRY TO DO THIS WHEN INFECTED BY *S. SOLIDUS!*

Look at how large *S. solidus* grows inside a stickleback!

REPRODUCE, SPREAD, REPEAT

Once a bird eats an infected stickleback, it infects itself with *S. solidus*. *S. solidus* grows a bit more and develops fully into an adult.

S. solidus often waits for a **mate** to reproduce, but it doesn't have to! *S. solidus* can reproduce all on its own. Depending on the size of the tapeworm, it will produce 12,000 to 20,000 eggs or more. These are spread by the host bird's waste. More copepods and sticklebacks are infected soon after.

TAKE-OVER TRUTHS

S. SOLIDUS ISN'T OFTEN LIVING OUTSIDE OF A HOST, SO IT DOESN'T HAVE ANY PREDATORS OF ITS OWN.

Bird waste is a great way for *S. solidus* to spread its eggs. Since birds fly, *S. solidus* might find a new body of water to start infecting!

RE PARASITES GOOD?

When there are parasites in an **ecosystem**, that shows the ecosystem is healthy. If parasites are missing, it often means something is wrong. The number of hosts could be decreasing, leaving the parasites with fewer to infect. Pollution is a major cause of these kinds of problems.

In this way, the zombie fish created by *S. solidus* are a good thing. Their presence lets us know a water ecosystem is doing fine. However harmful a parasite might seem, each has its place in nature.

THE LIFE CYCLE OF S. SOLIDUS

copepod eats
S. solidus larvae

larvae hatch
from the eggs
in the water

stickleback
eats infected
copepod

eggs leave the
bird in its waste

S. solidus's body
changes and grows

S. solidus finishes
developing and
produces eggs

stickleback begins to
swim alone and
in warmer waters

bird eats
stickleback

GLOSSARY

behavior: the way an animal acts

chemical: matter than can be mixed with other matter to cause changes

crustacean: an animal with a hard shell, jointed limbs, feelers, and no backbone

develop: to grow and change over time

digestive system: all the body parts concerned with eating, breaking down, and taking in food

ecosystem: all the living things in an area

hatch: to break open or come out of

infect: to spread inside the body

mate: one of two animals that come together to produce babies

organism: a living thing

reproduction: the act of an animal creating another creature just like itself

spine: one of many stiff, pointed parts growing from an animal

FOR MORE INFORMATION

BOOKS

Larson, Kirsten. *Zombies in Nature*. Mankato, MN: Amicus, 2016.

Lewis, Clare. *Fish Body Parts*. Chicago, IL: Capstone Heinemann Library, 2016.

WEBSITES

Relationships Between Organisms
www.biology4kids.com/files/studies_relationships.html
Read about how organisms interact, including parasites and hosts.

Three-Spined Stickleback
www.arkive.org/three-spined-stickleback/ gasterosteus-aculeatus-aculeatus/
Learn all about the fish that's zombified by *Schistocephalus solidus!*

INDEX